Cat Facts

Name:

Type/Breed:

Size:

Boy or Girl:

Color of fur:

Color of eyes:

Character:

Favorite food:

Favorite toy:

Funny habits:

There is a space below each picture frame where you can write your own caption, or you can copy the one we've written.

Photo tips

1. Ask an adult to show you how to use the camera if you are unsure.

2. Make sure you are using film for prints and not transparencies (slides).

3. When taking pictures outside remember to aim the camera away from the sun.

4. Check through the viewfinder to see that shadows do not hide your pet's features.

5. Remember that if your pet has a white coat you should look for a dark background, and vice versa.

6. Don't try to get too close to your pet or the photograph will not be in focus.

7. A picture taken at eye level with your pet will help you better capture its personality.

8. Wait until your pet is sitting or lying still. It is difficult to keep your pet in focus when it is running around.

9. Try to avoid using the flash near your pet's face. Its eyes are likely to come out red in the photograph and, more important, you may frighten your pet.

10. When you have come to the end of a roll, you must wind it back completely before you open the back of the camera to take it out.

11. Remember you will not get perfect pictures every time. Even experienced pet photgraphers may get only one or two great shots in a roll of film.

Stick photo here

It didn't take my cat long
to feel at home.

Stick photo here

What a cute face!
Here my cat is looking straight
at the camera . . .

4

Stick photo here

. . . and this is what my cat looks like
from the side.

Stick photo here

This is my favorite picture of kitty.
Isn't it cute?!

Stick photo here

Discovering things around
the house is a real adventure.
My cat is a great explorer!

Stick photo here

My cat loves eating and always
cleans the plate!

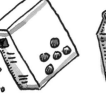

Stick photo here

. . . sweet dreams . . . sweet dreams . . . sweet
dreams . . . sweet dreams . . .

Stick photo here

My cat and I are the best of
friends. Here we are together!

Stick photo here

My cat has lots of toys.

Stick photo here

When we play in the garden, I find it
hard to keep up with my cat!

Stick photo here

My cat can fit almost anywhere!

Stick photo here
My cat does not like visiting the vet!

Stick photo here

I groom my cat's coat every day because
Mom hates fur on the furniture!

Stick photo here

My cat likes to sniff the
spring flowers.

Stick photo here

In summer, my cat stretches out
in a shady spot.

Stick photo here

My cat loves chasing leaves in the fall.

Stick photo here

In the winter when it is cold, I think my cat is lucky to have such a warm coat!

Stick photo here

My cat has lots of animal friends.

Stick photo here

My cat was just as excited
about the presents as I was!

Stick photo here
"On vacation" at the vet's!

Stick photo here

Muddy pawprints are a sign that
my cat has been out and about.

Stick photo here

My cat's bell warns the birds of danger!